Metamorphosis

by Vergie Lesea

METAMORPHOSIS

Poetry by
Vergie Lesea

Inspired by
A Course In Miracles
("ACIM")

Metamorphosis is a compilation of
original poems by Virginia Lesea.

Cover and interior graphics
by Isabell VanMerlin

ISBN-13: 978-1516854622

ISBN-10: 1516854624

This book is available from:
createspace.com/5671562
Amazon.com
and from most booksellers

The publishing of this little book of poems happened because I shared them with my son, Dennis.

Dennis, in turn, shared them with A Course in Miracles group in Sacramento, CA. Several members of this group agreed that they should be published and one member, Jean Ross, offered to type them, in order, for me. Another friend of mine, Frances Landcaster, offered to help and referred me to Michael Terranova; Michael referred me to Cheryl Dutton to put them in form for publishing and Isabell VanMerlin has finished the job and made the cover. My daughter, Sue Yesilada, has always been very encouraging. I feel a great sense of gratitude to all of these people.

I dedicate this book to my children Ron, John, Dennis, Austin and Sue Lesea Yesilada; my grandchildren Diane Benge, Jennifer Lesea-Ames, Karen Sudre, Sharda Ryan, Hira Lesea, Renee Lesea Johnson, Becki Lesea, Sermin Yesilada Breaden, and Selin Cronkrite. Also to my great-grandchildren Christina Lesea, Victoria Benge, Benjamin Lesea Pringle, Alanna Ryan, Evan Sudre, Elia Sudre, and Matthew Breaden, and my great-great-grandson, Beau Hickey. Also to my five sisters Vera Seifert, Opal Stolberg, Carma Mercer, Nelda Miller and Dawn Lucien; to many other relatives; and to all ACIM students all over the world.

My Spiritual Journey

As a child I always felt that the Universe was taking care of me. Of course my Mother and Father (Hazel and Austin Sharp) did their loving part.

When I was 18 years of age I read *Sermon On The Mount* by Emmet Fox and *The Power Of Positive Thinking* by Noman Vincent Peale. These books brought me to a new way of thinking.

For several years I attended Unity Church and in the early 1970's I took two correspondence courses from Unity. It was during this period that a few of these poems came to me.

In 1982, I discovered A Course In Miracles and attended many groups in California, the Bay Area and in Oregon. This material spoke to me at a different level. For years I did the lessons and reading every day. Many times I went to a "Miracles Camp" for a week. Most of this poetry was inspired by A Course In Miracles (ACIM).

CONTENTS

METAMORPHOSIS

Escaping From the Chrysalis

If we enter daily our cocoon
And stay in silence there
We will emerge the butterfly
Free to fly and soar.

I Am Precious In His Sight

I am precious in His sight
Like a lovely, priceless jewel
With many facets of the Light
Clearly shining through
I am loved so very dearly
More than words can express,
I remember I'm Your Child
Your gift to me is happiness.

In The Stillness

In the stillness, in the quiet,
In that special inner place,
I remember, for a moment,
To return, to find that space.
Just a very small beginning
That is all it ever takes
The rest is all done for me
By His gift of perfect Grace.

My New Frontier

While others concentrate on the
exploration of outer space
My search is for inner space.
It's not "out there,"
It's not "somewhere,"
It's all contained within.
I sally forth on the most
   expanding,
The most revealing,
The greatest journey of all
To find the magnificent galaxy
   within me.

The Inner Court

I enter into the inner court
With praise and thanksgiving,
In gratitude I sing with joy!
I feel love enfolding me.
Waves of peace wash over me
Acting like a buoy,
Floating on the wings of love,
Treasured forever
Lifted high above.

He Speaks To Me

In the silence, in the stillness
In the hush of Heaven
His Voice speaks to me
Not just seventy times seven
But times without number
As I still the thunder
Of my thinking mind.

The Upside Down World

The world I see is upside down,
A topsy-turvy view,
For truth and knowledge are
    within,
A different hue.
Color me purple, color me red,
The mind seems to say,
When all the time the color's
    there
Its own special ray.

The Ancient Memory

An ancient memory, an ancient
  call
Is sounding in the altar of my
  heart.
It is beating out the rhythm of
  love.
It is reverberating in the
  atmosphere
that surrounds me,
Filling me with gratitude and
  admiration
For the Holiness within us all.

Healing

I see you whole and unafraid
In your heart the Heart of God is
    laid
Your perfection shines so clear,
A vision of joy, health and cheer.
Child of God, accept His gifts,
Accept your Holiness, accept the
    bliss,
As our minds are healed it's true
Your complete expression comes
    shining through.

The Ancient Song

I choose to remember the
    ancient song
Singing its glad refrain in me,
The rhythm beats within my
    heart--
The notes play upon my mind--
How dear and lovely is the
    melody,
Making my life a symphony.

Freeing the Barriers

The barriers I've erected
Built solidly and strong
Can be dispelled and ejected
By the lasering of Love.
They seem firmly formed
Like granite or rock.
But they are only an attitude of
   mind.
So I remember the flip-flop
Of a thought:
From anger to peace,
From tears to release,
From fear to Love.

Love Or Fear?

Is it love I'm expressing
Or is it fear?
One or the other
I do hold dear.
The choice is mine
I always choose.
Love is to gain,
Fear is to lose.
To fulfill my destiny
I remember my Divinity.

Freedom

I am free to soar like an eagle
Free to fly like a dove,
Free to skim over the water
Free to float above
All limitation.
Praise God, I am Free to be
All that I was meant to be.

A Vision

I see a new Heaven and a new
  earth
A new world-- a new birth,
The birth of sight and love and
  light,
Forgiveness shining-- brilliant--
  bright;
Glorious, marvelous, joyous day;
Heaven's reflection, casting its
  ray
Into the depths of my
  consciousness.

A Prayer

Holy Essence, Love Divine,
Let me see into my mind.
Reveal to me each tiny thought
That is bringing me to naught.
Lead me, guide me every day,
Inward, onward, this I pray.
Release me, free me, make me
    clear,
Sparking, shining, full of cheer.

My Purpose

My only purpose, my only goal,
To learn to live my perfect role,
To accept God's Love, give up
    fear,
Let inner guidance be so clear,
So I can express Love to
    everyone
And let His Holy Will be done.

Awakening

The sun is shining
On the horizon of my heart
The night is over,
Love I now impart.
The flame is burning--
The light is beaming--
The dispelling of the dark.

My Part

I have a part to play,
A function, a role.
I'm part of God's plan
My true and only goal---
To see others as mirrors
reflecting to me
Whatever it is I need to see.

I Am As God Created Me

I am as God created me
Always--- forever--- eternally.
I am the same
Holy--- whole--- perfect
That's my Name.
I'm finished with the worldly
  game;
I accept my true role
In God's heavenly domain.

The Bridge Of Forgiveness

There is a bridge
It is built by man
It is the bridge of forgiveness.
I step up and cross the span
I now walk from
Anxiety to peace
Illusion to Reality
Humanity to Divinity.

In Gratitude

In gratitude and thankfulness
In awe and wonder---
I bow down before my Creator,
Knowing that I already am
And have all I'll ever need.
It is planted in the seed,
It is established in my mind.
I accept and use it now.

Come To You

I come with open heart and open
    mind
To the Father, within, and there
    I find
The gifts of joy, of peace, and
    bliss
Of Love's reflection, and the kiss
Of heaven.

The Open Door

Beneath my senseless thoughts I
    find
An open door within my mind,
A deep and lasting reservoir
Heaven's storehouse, safe and
    secure,
I open wide this door of Light,
Let His Eyes give me sight,
All I've ever known I remember,
Now I can express His Love, so
    tender.

Memory

Take my memory back
Over the experiential track
To that place of Love and peace.
Let my mind be so filled
That the memory be spilled
Into my awareness.

I Am Worthy

I am worthy!
Not because of my numerous
  deeds.
I am worthy
Because of the miraculous seeds
Of worthiness planted in me
From the beginning of time.
This is my reason and rhyme
As I accept Holiness as mine
I am worthy.

Celebration

Sing--- express--- shout it out!
The good news of our Divinity!
Move--- dance--- pirouette--
Express individuality.
WE are the song---
We are the story---
We are the dance---
Expressing our glory!

The Dream

I am the dreamer, I am the
  dream,
It's not someone else's plot or
  scheme.
I take the first step---
Look at Cause and effect.
They aren't different, they are
  the same,
I make it up--- I make the game.
I now see clearly, I now see past
the dream I made. It will not
  last;
I choose to see another view
Change my mind, see anew
Accept the "happy dream" as
  mine
Step into Light and let it shine.

A Vision

I keep my sight forever focused
On the pure and guiding Light.
I see all people loving---joyful;
Free from fear---rejoicing---
   bright;
Each one helping every other
Treating all mankind as one.
Free from judgment---
   condemnation,
Knowing Spirit's work is done.
A world that knows no pain or
   illness
Using Love to communicate
Celebrating every meeting;
Joining--- this is our fate.

His Most Precious Gifts

He give me silence,
He gives me peace;
He gives me Holiness,
    remembered.
He gives me vision,
He gives me Love,
He gives me all I've ever
    treasured.

I Am Willing

I am willing to release
All of my past thoughts and
    emotions;
For there is no gain
in holding on to pain.
Your Will for me is perfect
    happiness.
I gladly give up my quest
And accept Your wondrous joy.
    (gift)

It Only Takes A Moment

It only takes a moment to
remember Who I am,
It only takes a moment to be
Spiritual Woman.
A second of love--- an instant of
peace---
A twinkling of joy--- a sudden
release.
A snap of the finger of God in my
consciousness.

I Choose This Day

I choose this day to hear
The Holy Spirit speak
Of beauty, joy, of oneness;
Of the healing of perception.

I choose this hour to hear
The Holy Spirit speak
Of Truth, of peace, of love;
Of knowing, of perfection.

I choose this moment to hear
The holy Spirit speak
For He speaks healingly
Lovingly, eternally--- now.

Open My Heart

Holy Spirit, open my heart
to more of Your Love,
More of Your grace,
Take over my inner space.

Peal off the layers of doubt,
Help me to shed
All I fear and dread;
And learn to live in
Each golden moment of eternity;
Just to be.

Effervescence

I invoke the Holy Christ Light
To bubble up from my inmost
　　center,
To effervesce into all areas
Of my Beingness.
To heal, to bless, to inspire;
To illumine, to balance, to
　　empower;
To manifest all the love and
　　harmony
That are mine to share;
To open my eyes, to clear my
　　perception;
Thank You, Christ Light for
　　perfect expression.

What Do I Want ?

I want with all my heart and
  mind
To know Your Voice and how to
  find
Your peace, Your grace, Your
  Truth, Your Light,
To feel Your Love, to have Your
  sight,
To know Your touch, Your joy,
  Your bliss
To feel Heaven's gentle kiss
On my consciousness.

Miracles Camp *1987*

The fresh air, the cool breeze,
The beauty of nature
Brings me to my knees
In adoration;
The kisses, the hugs,
The welcoming love
The beauty of humanity
Causes me to shout
In exultation.

Listening

Right now is the time I will
   listen and hear
The Voice for God, so soft and
   clear;
I'll keep an open mind and
   attentive ear
Tuned to the higher frequency
Of the Almighty Endless Sound.
I am reminded each precious
   instant
That God is speaking, teaching,
   loving me.

Turning Within

I turn within and there I find
The total Love within my mind
And in the very heart of me
The Love and Light that set me
    free!
Becoming quiet, becoming still
Listening with all my will.
Let my mind be so filled
That the memory be spilled
Into my consciousness.

Freeing The Barriers

Past the clouds of doubt and
    confusion-
Past the barriers of guilt and
    fear-
Taking His Hand to guide me-
Knowing His Love inside me-
I move through the mist and all
    is clear.

Beyond Thought

Beyond words, beyond thought,
Beyond the symbols in my mind
There is a place in me I find
A deep and lasting reservoir,
The very Center---the very core,
Here I do find more and more
Peace, love, strength and bliss,
Here I feel the kiss of Heaven
On my soul.

Beyond Thought #2

Beyond thought, beyond words,
Beyond the symbols in my mind
There is a place in me I find;
It's always here--- a memory
    clear-
A sense of joy, a sense of peace-
An inner laughter waiting
    release-
A sense of Love--- abiding, deep-
I touch it now, it feels complete.

Perception

What I am seeing is not what it
  appears to be
I have taken it all and turned it
  topsy-turvy,
Upside down and inside out,
Trying to figure what it's all
  about;
Thank God, I do not know,
But there is One Who does.
I give it all to Him
And simply bask in His love.

A New World

In meditation I climb
To the mountain top and find
A panoramic view-
A world that's new;
A world surrounded and
   sustained
In heavenly light, exchanged
For all the fears that I have
   known;
Each thought of fear and
   sadness goes
As brilliance replaces each form
A new world ---- reborn.

Help From Nature

I let the sun remind me
  of the availability of all
  energy---
I let the light of the stars
  illumine
  my mind with clear thinking---
I let the moon balance my
  emotions
  as it balances the ebb and flow
  of the tide-
I let the beauty of the mountain
  top
  lift my aspirations to the
  summit and above-
I let the many faces of the
  flowers
  remind me of the many faces
  of mankind-

I let the view of the horizon
  broaden my view as I look
  beyond-
I let the changing of the night to
  day
  remind me of the balance of
  the Universe.

Nature

I've wandered in on nature's
    habitat
But I don't feel like an intruder.
For I have learned to listen
  to the sounds of nature stirring
  to the voice of Spirit moving
Cross the pathway of my heart.

The Role

Are you open and willing to
    accept
Who you really are?
Are you ready to perform
  as the brilliant star?
The stage is set---
The curtain rises---
Enter center stage---now!

Holy Essence

Holy essence, Holy fire,
Burning brighter hour by hour-
Flame up in me and consume
Everything that's not in tune
   with all the heavenly, Holy
   bliss-
Clear away the foggy mist;
The fire of love is brightly
   burning-
Shining, radiant, brilliant,
   glowing-
My heart's on fire with heavenly
   fervor
As I touch the Holiness of the
   tremor
      in my soul.

Teach Only Love

Teach only love for this is what
    we are
Love's radiance is brighter than
    a star
It's found within, and never from
    afar,
Seek only love for this is what
    we are.

Teach only love for this is our
    Truth within
It shines so bright it never will
    grow dim
The time is now so let us all
    begin
Teach only love for this is our
    Truth within.

Teach only love and let it start
  to grow.
The more we teach the more
  that it will glow
We sense it now and let it really
  flow
Teach only love for this is all we
  know.

Christ Light

Oh, Holy Christ Light within
Break through the fear that
   binds,
Free me forever from my chains
And still my searching mind.

The Way To Forgiveness

Forgiveness is completely letting
   go
Of each and every thought
What have they ever brought
But pain and suffering and
   tears?
I gladly let go of my fears,
   Let Love enter in and here
   remain
As I stand fast in God's domain.
My mind forever being sane.

Guilt

The guilt is not in you, the
  guilt's in me,
The Holy Spirit set us free;
I see my very Self guiltless and
  pure,
A Child of God I am, I'm very
  sure,
I see my very Self guiltless and
  pure.

The Holy Spirit works within my
  mind
To set me free from guilt
Leave cares behind;
To sail beyond the mind to isles
  of peace,
Therein to find my Self and
  know release.

Mountain Top

On mountain top I stand serene
While all about me dance unseen
The forms and figures in the
   dream
Vague shadows now across the
   screen.

The play of thought within my
   mind
Is not so difficult to find,
I let it go---release it all,
Now that I've heard His
   wondrous call
"Return to me".

A Different World

I choose to see a different world
A world I really want
Where truth and freedom are
  expressed
In every word, in every thought;
 A world where love and endless
  joy
Are all that's ever taught.

Light

There is no darkness---
Every corner of my mind
  Is swept clear of all debris;
Only light shines clear and free
The lasering effect of light
Removes all darkness;
I let it shine everywhere
In every thought--- in every
  space---
In every experience--- in every
  face.

Memory Of His Love

The memory of His love returns
   to me
And activates the love in me
Changes my mind totally;
I forgive everything that isn't
   Love, joy and peace;
I let it all go---release
It all to Love.

Free

I am limitless---free---unbound,
 Loosened forever from the
   chains of fear
   That seemed to wrap me
   round.
   Free of all limits, safe and
   whole and healed
Living forever in His Love Light
   Field.

Going Past Fear

Past the clouds of doubt and
   confusion
Past the barriers of my fear
There's a light so bright, nothing
   can hide,
It dissolves my inner tears.

Love parts the clouds, lets light
   shine through
Love brushes all my fears aside,
Love answers every single doubt,
On Love's great wave I now do
   ride.

The Face Of Divinity

I take His Hand, He leads me on
Over all the rough and rocky
    places,
His love lifts me high above
He shows me all my many faces,
Until my One Face is revealed to
    me
The Face of true Divinity.

Remembering God

I am loved, protected, safe,
Held forever in God's warm
  embrace,
At peace within my heart;
Feeling His strength, we're
  never apart,
Expressing joy I start
Each day with remembrance of
  Him.

God's Love

God's Love wraps me round
Like an afghan on a cool
   evening,
Like a warm breeze fanning me,
Like the sun shining on my
   shoulder,
Like a warm cascading waterfall
Each drop caressing me,
Like loving arms cradling me in
   their fold,
Like His hand in mine guiding
   me,
Like His Voice telling me He
   loves me.

I Am Free

Free as a bird on the wing
Now my heart can sing
And dance and shout
Now I know what I'm about,
Free--- free--- free---
Of all that I have made.
    I've played it out.

A Lighted Path

He leads me down a lighted path
He guides my steps aright
He tells me where to go, whom
    to see,
And gives me strength and light.
In quietness, so softly,
    He speaks to me of sight.
An inner knowing, and inner
    voice,
He tells me everything's all
    right.

When I Am In Joy

When in joy I spend each day
I know Holy Spirit guides my
    way,
As unconditional love I express
I know that I am truly blessed,
I see holiness in everyone
Seeing them all as the perfect
    Son.

To Family and Friends

In gratitude and thankfulness
In awe and wonder
I fall on bended knee
In honor of your Divinity!
  You are magnificent!
  You are wondrous!
  You are an example of
  perfection!
I appreciate and celebrate your
  Holiness!

Reciprocal Love

My love for God---His love for me
Is reciprocal--- totally,
There is no place where His love
   starts
And mine begins,
There is only love.

Are You Willing?

Are you open and willing
To accept Who you really are?
Are you ready to perform
As the brilliant star?
The stage is set, the lights are
   on,
The curtain rises----
Enter center stage---now!

"Today I Forget All Things Except Your Love"

(Lesson 346 ACIM)

It always lifts me high above
All my doubts and all my fears;
Love lifts me into another
   dimension
Away from all anxiety and
   tension,
Love makes of my mind an open
   space
Helping me receive God's Love
   and grace.

God's Voice

Today I come in silence to hear
  God's Voice
and His alone;
His shining love for me He's
  shown
His strength, His guidance,
Whisper to me now,
Revealing to me the way and the
  how
To know with all my heart and
  my mind
I no longer need, I simply find.

Voice For God

Today I ask to hear God's Voice
    and His Alone
I quiet all my thoughts and
    theories
And let my mind return to His
    throne
Of endless love that frees me
From the prison of stone
That I have made.

I Am Love

In the very depths of me
In my very Essence
Love is my very Beingness
Love is my very Presence.

We Are One

Your joy is my joy
Your pain is my pain;
We aren't different
We are the same.
Your hurts, your anger,
Your love, your peace
Are in me to lessen or increase
Your experience is mine as well,
We make it Heaven or we make
   it hell.

Watching My Thoughts

I project my thought upon a
   screen
And watch them drift on by
For I do not know what they
   mean
And I'm not going to try
To figure everything all out
What a waste of time;
For peace is found between the
   thoughts
Where everything is mine;
In the gap, in the space
Between the thoughts is Grace.

Be The Queen

Take now your seat on the
  throne
Put on the Royal crown,
The flowing robe, the crested
  ring,
You are the Queen.

God's Treasure House

I enter His treasure house where
        all is healed
Each and every need already
        fulfilled;
Before I call I receive the
        treasure---
Pressed down, running over,
    more than I can measure.

I Am Listening

With all my heart and mind I
  want
To hear God's Voice, to be
  taught,
To let His Voice
Re-think my every thought,
Reinterpret my pet theories,
Open my mind to the Truth that
  frees
me from all opinions, beliefs and
  stories.
Oh, what a glorious release
I am listening.

He Touched Me

He touched me.
I still feel His hand on my
    shoulder
I still feel His touch on my brow;
I am energized, I am transported
Into the very now,
Every cell and atom alive
And tingling with energy
Transformation at a cellular
    level
Now I can truly BE!

What Do I Want?

I want a quiet heart, a peaceful
   mind,
To know where to look and how
   to find
My inner joy, my inner peace,
My greatest desire, to know
   release.
I'm not the victim, I'm the victor
As I remember to turn more and
   more
To Holy Spirit which takes me to
   the Core.

The Giver, The Gift

I am the giver, I am the gift
Now is the time I make the shift,
To give love in every situation
And witness my transformation.

I Am Worthy

I am worthy!
Not because of my numerous
   deeds.
I am worthy because of the seeds
Of worthiness planted in me
From the beginning of time.
There really is a reason and
   rhyme
A gift for all time
As I accept Holiness as mine.
I am worthy!

Forgiveness

The guilt is not in you, the
  guilt's in me;
Holy Spirit will set me free.
I can see myself guiltless and
  pure
A child of God I am, I'm very
  sure.

Holy Spirit works within my
  mind
To set me free from guilt,
Leave cares behind.
To sail beyond my mind to isles
  of peace
Therein to find my Self and
  know release.

Desire

With all my heart and mind
It's Your Voice I want to find,
I want Your guidance constantly
To hear You answer lovingly;
To be so quiet, to be so still,
To hear Your message, to know
  Your Will;
To feel Your Love expressing
  through
As I return my Love to You.

God's Voice

Today I ask to hear Your Voice
  and Yours alone.
I quiet all my thoughts and
  theories
And let my mind return to Your
  throne
Of endless Love that frees me
From the prison of stone I have
  made.

He Leads Me

He leads me down a lighted path
And guides my steps aright,
He tells me where to go and
   whom to see
He gives me strength and light;
In quietness, so softly,
He speaks to me of sight,
An inner knowing, and inner
   view
That says everything's all right.

A Different World

I choose to see a different world
   A world I really want;
Where truth and freedom are
   expressed
   In every act, in every thought;
A world where endless love and
   joy
   Are all that's ever taught.

Open My Heart

In the quiet, in the stillness
In the sweet embracing place
I touch Your Grace
Your Love filled space
That dissolves the line that
    divides
And hides our Oneness.
Take over my inner space.
Peel off the layers, help me to
    shed
all that I dread;
Help me to live each golden
    moment
with you in Eternity,
Just to BE!

Quietness

There is a place in me that's
   quiet
   There is a place in me that's
   still,
There is a place in me of perfect
   peace,
   Deep silence---so tranquil;

There is a place in me of total
   strength,
And trust and light and Love,
There is a place in me where
Nothing is impossible or above
 accomplishment.

As I Remember Love

As I remember Love every
   second of every day
And translate everything I see
   into Love's array
I watch the barriers I've built to
   Love
Fall away.

The Love Of God

I know and feel His Love in
    every fiber
I feel my heart opening wider
    and wider
To accept His every caress,
To extend, to heal, to bless;
I forgive every thought I've ever
    had
Of pain, of limit, of so-called
    "bad;"
I'm open and I do expand
    Into His Love and here I
    stand.

I See You

I see you free and unafraid
Your mind on God forever
   stayed.
I see you bright, shining, clear,
Free of strain and free of fear;
I see your path ahead is straight
Light is shining through an open
   gate,
And through this gate you're
   gently led,
All shackles and chains forever
   shed;
Energy flows to you from above
   You are Light and you are
   Love.

Christ Light

I invoke the Holy Christ Light
To bubble up from my inmost
  center
To effervesce into all areas
Of my Beingness.
To heal, to bless, to inspire;
To illumine, to balance, to
  empower;
To manifest all the love and
  harmony
That are mine to share;
To open my mind, to clear my
  perception
Thank You, Christ Light, for
  perfect expression.

Appreciation

In appreciation and adoration
My feelings soar in exultation
Your Altar of Love rises higher
  and higher
Within my heart it becomes my
  desire;
You speak the word, I hear Your
  call
I see only Holiness and Love in
  all.

A Prayer For Healing

There is a Light in you more
  powerful
  than any physical symptom.

This Light is so bright it shines
  away
  everything that is unlike It.

It zeros in on any aspect to
  dissolve it
  into Its nothingness.

Love joins the Light and is
  magnified
  a billion times

And then a billion more.

You are the Light.

You are the Love.

You are healed.

From Thinking To Being

It's not "out there"
It's not somewhere.
It's all contained within.
It's not "someone"
It's everyone,
A Light that never does grow
   dim.
It's a silent state, a love filled
   place,
A tranquil, unformed space
Of simply being What we are!

The Dawning

When the Light dawns in my
  mind
Every corner of my Beingness is
  illumined.
There are no dark places.
All is Light!
It does reveal the Truth of What
  I am,
A priceless jewel---- a gem,
A pulsating ball of energy,
A luminous, resplendent
  Divinity.

My Self

My "self" is nothing, my "Self" is
    all,
Remembering this I hear Your
    call,
I know Your Love and gentle
    care
Are always with me,
    everywhere.
Your Voice forever leads and
    guides
I find It now, deep inside,
Telling me all I need to know
Forever remembering to let Love
    show.

Prayer For Wholeness

I call upon Holy Spirit in my
   mind
to bring to my awareness
the Truth of Who and What I
   really am.
The laws of God work only for
   my good,
and nothing but the laws of God
are working in my life.
I accept my value, my
   wholeness, my Divinity.
The Great Rays are shining in
   my mind
Dissolving every thought that is
   not perfection.

Holy Spirit leads and guides me
to my natural, original state of
   peace.
In my heart the Heart of God is
   laid,
In my mind the Mind of God is
   made clear.
When the Light shines in, there
   is no darkness.
Every corner of my Mind is
   shining with Holiness.

Eternal Dawn

Past the clouds of doubt and
   confusion,
Past the images of fear,
There is a light so bright it
   cannot hide
It shines brilliantly and clear.
I take His Hand, He leads me on
Past all the barriers I have
   made;
I enter now this healing Light,
I bathe in this eternal dawn.

God's Presence Within

I want with all my heart and
   mind
To sense and KNOW God's
   Presence--- To find IT
As near and close as my very
   breath.
A personal relationship with
   Jesus.
One on One, day to day,
Moment to moment,
Heart to heart,
Take over my life, my mind my
   body,
Take over ME.
Here in my inmost Center
He is my very heart beat.

With All My Heart

With all my heart and mind
I want to find
To know and experience Him
The perpetual chuckle---the
   endless grin
Eternal Joy---deep within.
Every second, every moment
Knowing All that's meant
For me to have and to be
Just Holy Me.

Into His Presence

Forgiveness leads me to the gate
Gratitude lets me enter
Love takes me into the Inner
   Court
To the very Center
Of His Presence

Transformation

I touch Love in the stillness
I will never again be the same!
For I've touched my very Is-ness
And I'm transformed into
What I've always been!

Nothing Can Change
Eternal Love

I've never left His endless Love
I'm still in His embrace
His gentle kiss upon my brow
His touch upon my face;
His arms so quietly enfold
They lift me up on wings,
His angels flock about me now
In choir as they sing
"Nothing can change eternal
    Love."

Oneness

One breath breathed deeply
One mind opened freely
One heart expanding greatly
One love that's total.

Some Christmas Poems

Christmas

The star is the Light shining in
    every man.
It is within us and not afar;
The shepherds are our gentle
    thoughts
That recognize this star.
The manger is the place
    prepared
Within our consciousness
For the birth of Love this very
    day
As we realize our Oneness.

Where Is The Child?

"Where is the Child?" you ask
    from afar.
Follow the Light, follow the star.
It comes to rest right where you
    are
In the manger of your heart
The Child gets Its start.

The New Birth

This is the season
Reminding us of the reason
For the birth of the Child within.
Starting in a lowly manger
Feeling like a lonesome stranger
Rising out of the dream
Into the throne of Divinity
Let the Holy Child rule supreme.

Christmas Gifts

With each gift we wrap this
   season
We're reminded of the reason
For this glorious celebration.
We wrap each one in Love
Tie it with a ribbon of peace
And decorate it with joy!

Remembrance

Amid the hustle and bustle
Of the Christmas season
Stop, and remember the reason
Over two thousand years ago
An Angel Man came to show
us how to love without exception
no rejection----only Love.

IN A LIGHTER VEIN

The Redwood Tree

Your strength, your energy, your
  endurance
Give me the reassurance
Of God's Love everywhere;
You spread your branches to
  make shade,
Protected now, I'm not afraid.
I breathe in your aroma,
I feel the sun's rays filtering
  through,
You embrace me, I embrace you;
For one brief moment
I sense our oneness.

I Have A Little Ego

I have a little ego that goes
  everywhere with me
And what can be her purpose is
  more than I can see,
She is very like me from her feet
  up to her head
And she gets me into trouble
  because she sees all red.
Ego- ego- wherever I go--- she go.
This morning very early when it
  was still quite dark
I thought that I was free of her,
  I'd left her in the park,
But later as I talked to my dear
  friend on the phone
Very soon I realized that I was
  not alone.
Ego- ego- wherever I go--- she go.
She always likes to tell me that
  I'm not good enough,

There's no way I can do it and a
   lot of other "stuff,"
She likes to get me sad and in a
   mournful mood,
To remember all my errors and
   on these to brood.
Ego-ego-wherever I go---she go.
But finally I remember there is
   help for me,
 Spirit tells me "Call on Me,
   you'll see,"
And so I ask for certainty and a
   different view
And all my dreams are
   vanished—I can see anew.
Ego-ego--- Spirit gives the
   "heave ho."

What God Is Not!

God is not a puppeteer
Pulling strings to watch us
    dance,
God is not a fabricator,
God is not a manipulator.

God is not a leprechaun
Playing tricks to watch us
    squirm,
God is not an aggravator,
God is not an agitator.

God doesn't have a dividing line
Choosing between the good and
    bad,
God is not an analyzer,
God is not a reciprocator.

God doesn't have a book of
  records
Keeping track of all we do,
God is not a formulator,
God is not an evaluator.

Manipulator, agitator,
Analyzer, evaluator,
These are all a childish plot.
I hope I know what God is NOT!

Sisters

Oh, the joy of having sisters
Loving, sharing all we can,
Helping, trusting, corresponding
Keeping in touch with each
one.

Wishing, hoping, praying, caring
Sending blessings on their
way,
Remembering all our special
meetings
Fondly, sweetly, everyday.

Help Me Remember

The "aye" in aim,
The "go" in goal,
The "purr" in purpose,
And the "fun" in function

Mt. Hood

(My first view of Mt. Hood from
my condo)

There it stood---- Mt. Hood!
In all its glorious array!
It greeted me this day
Bathed in the colors of the
    sunrise
In all of their resplendent hue,
What a spectacular view!

Mt. Rainier

As I look at the mountain
    I reach out with my thoughts
    To embrace and enfold it
    I draw it close to me
And it becomes an integral part
    of me.

OLDER POETRY

Thoughts

If we could but grasp the power
Of the thoughts we hold in mind
We would be extremely careful
Of the quality and kind
Of thoughts we choose to dwell
  upon
and thoughts that really don't
  belong
In the substance of our mind.

The Answer

I struggled, concentrated,
strained, contemplated,
Thought deeply, even meditated.
"Where are the results?" I asked.
The answer came ----
"You have only to accept and
   know."

Back

Take my memory back
Over the experiential track
To the place of love and light,
Let my mind be so filled
That the memory be spilled
Into my awareness.

Attitude

There are only two main
  attitudes.
They consist of 'yea' and 'nay,'
These attitudes of mind appear
In all we do and all we say.

Whatever the need, whatever
  the plan
We either accept or reject,
Wherever we are, whatever we
  do
We either absorb or reflect.

In affairs of the heart of affairs
  of the world
We join with or refrain from.
The results always show and
  appear in our lives
As that which we think we
  become.

Now

Why wait 'til the hereafter
To attain celestial joy?
The thrill is in the doing
In each moment of the day!

There are sixty seconds in every
    minute
Sixty minutes in every hour
Any moment you can reach
The top window of the tower.

So rejoice and live life fully,
Make the most of every day
Experience joy and laughter
Throughout your earthly stay.

Words

Take a word and ponder--
    concentrate
Think deeply--even meditate,
The power in the word is there
To cause that word to
    demonstrate.

Take a word and speak it softly.
Express it openly and realize,
The power is there
To cause that word to
    materialize.

Take a word and act the part,
    The performance is about to
    start,
Our bodies, lives, affairs and
    heart
Reveal to the world our words
    counterpart.

Only God

If I could but concentrate
On God alone and meditate,
Forgetting all the cons and pros,
Forgetting all the wise man
  knows,
Make of my mind an open
  vessel,
I wouldn't have to strain or
  wrestle,
I wouldn't care about the
  Masters,
I wouldn't have to find the
  answers,
For I would know without a
  doubt
What everything is all about.

This book was proofed and formatted by
Isabell's Text and Publishing
isabell.vanmerlin@verizon.net